M000028495

A CONVERSATION
WITH JESUS

ON

RELIGION

A CONVERSATION
WITH JESUS

ON

RELIGION

DAVID HELM

CHRISTIAN
FOCUS

ISBN 978-1-5271-0324-5

Published in 2019

by

Christian Focus Publications Ltd.,
Geanies House, Fearn, Ross-shire,
IV20 1TW, Great Britain

www.christianfocus.com

Cover design and typeset by: Pete Barnsley (CreativeHoot.com)

Printed in China

CONTENTS

TWO WORDS
BEFORE
BEGINNING

ONE

The book in your hands is one of six. Short volumes all. Think of them as people to meet, not pages to be read. In each, a charcoal sketch is drawn of a person who first appeared on the pages of John's Gospel. Both women and men. Real flesh and blood. All worthy of attention. And each one fully capable of standing on their own two feet.

Beyond this, they all have someone in common. Jesus. The Nazarene. The Christ— he who forever changed the world we live in. Anyway, they all met him. In person. And they talked with him. More than that. Each one had a *conversation with Jesus* about something important to them.

TWO

I suppose something should be said about why 'these six'? Let's just say the selection is subjective. Author's prerogative. I liked them. I wanted to know them. And I learned significant things from each one of them. There are good reasons to think that you will connect with them too. Their struggles are our struggles. Their questions too. In fact, some people are saying there has never been another century to resemble the one these six lived in, until ours came along. And if that is the case, you may just run into yourself by running into them.

At any rate, there came a day when they all ran into Jesus. Of course, he is the only character to emerge in every encounter. I am confident that you will enjoy getting to know him.

DIRECTOR'S
NOTES

CAST:

NICODEMUS: a Jewish leader, advanced in age, religiously dressed

JESUS: a younger teacher, with beard, and commonly attired

HOUSEHOLD SERVANT: nondescript in every way

SETTING:

An ordinary house, in a quiet first-century town in the Levant. An older, but distinguished looking man, approaches. The sun has recently set. Light from burning candles escapes the home as the door is pulled open to him.

The man introduces himself as Nicodemus. He says he has come in hopes of having a conversation with the one called Jesus. He is invited in and given a seat at the table. Some bread is set before him. The furnishings are sparse. The house servant leaves the room and a younger bearded man enters.

A CONVERSATION WITH JESUS ON
RELIGION

It is one thing to decide not to follow the teacher but quietly to go back home, which, after hearing the Sermon on the Mount, I would have done. It is another thing altogether to lose interest in what Jesus had to say. And I cannot imagine, living at that time, I could ever have lost interest.

— A RABBI TALKS WITH JESUS[1]

I can't help but think that Nicodemus would have thought our present-day discussions on religion to be strangely curious.

After all, he was a religious man.

We meet him on the pages of John's Gospel prior to his conversation with Jesus.[2]

> *Now there was a man of the* Pharisees *named Nicodemus,* a ruler of the Jews.

Pharisees were known for their devotion to the Hebrew Bible. They were people of the book, religionists—spending vast amounts of time studying the Law of Moses and applying it to life. In general, Pharisees were spiritually earnest. They went to synagogue regularly and they lived by the golden rule of treating others the way you want to be treated.

Yet, Nicodemus is also described as a *ruler of God's people*. This means that in addition to being a Pharisee, he would have been a member of the Sanhedrin. Comprised of seventy men, the Sanhedrin was charged with upholding Judaism's unique identity in an increasingly hostile first-century world. And as advocates for their religious freedom, they were responsible for Judaism's temple life with its proper worship of God.

In introducing Nicodemus to us in this way, John reveals that Nicodemus was grounded in religion, as both a pastor and protector of God's people. He was confident in his knowledge of God, and fixed in his belief that

God knew him. Put simply, his religion and relationship to God were inseparable.

RELIGIOUS CONFIDENCE

For Nicodemus, *religion* was something still important. He retained confidence in its inherent value. So much so that he would have been saddened by today's notion that the world would be a better place without it. After all, Nicodemus would have reasoned, 'Don't most religious people make positive contributions to society? Don't most of them serve their respective cities and communities? And don't they do it with humility and genuine interest in the common good?' For Nicodemus, the problem would not have been that we have too much religion, but that it is not the right kind. For him, religion connects us not only to God and the afterlife, but also to purposeful living now.

With a bit of imagination, we can picture ourselves alive in his day. Our paths might even have crossed. And if so, perhaps we would have been so bold as to ask him: 'Excuse me, sir, do you really feel such a need to put so much effort into religion? Is holding on to a religious belief even necessary anymore? Is that even advisable? After all, religion is often a source of violence, oppression and ongoing evil. Perhaps what we need is not freedom of religion, but freedom *from* religion? For you religionists (those who practice their religion) seem to being doing more harm than good.'

Turning toward us, and looking thoughtful, he may have said: 'I don't think I would put it quite like that. Yes, it is true that some stake holders in religion have done considerable damage, and many people have been subject to irreparable harm. And that demands repentance. But, and I say this with sincerity, that is not the case for us all. I am a religious man. I have a deep and personal faith. And I possess a deep trust in all that the Bible proclaims. But I remain confident that my religious convictions make the world a better place. In fact, if I may be so bold in response to you, *(still kind, but now almost in an accusatory tone)* be careful before you continue denigrating all religion and the religious. You could be in danger of committing blasphemy.'

All of this, and more, Nicodemus might have said. And we would have admired especially the tenor of his voice. Here is a humble man, we would have thought, yet also confident. Here is one who embodies the very real and continuing power of religious faith.

Yet, and this should surprise us, on the night Nicodemus knocked on the door of the home where Jesus was staying, Jesus would call into question all that confidence in religion which Nicodemus exuded. For Jesus, something was deficient in the way Nicodemus related to God and this world. He was religious, but yet, not in a right relationship with God. And this fact skewed everything to which he gave himself. To grasp this staggering claim (that one can be genuinely religious, morally upright and loving toward others, and yet, at the same time be off-putting to God), we first need to listen to the conversation they had, and especially how Jesus, a younger teacher than was Nicodemus, proved himself to be wise beyond his years.

CONFIDENCE IN RELIGION IS CHALLENGED

The Gospel of John tells us that it was Nicodemus, not Jesus, who began the conversation. 'Rabbi, we know that you are a teacher come from God, for no one can do these signs that you do unless God is with him.' This opening line, as we shall see, is loaded with religious subtlety. It possesses a hubris that Jesus will take issue with right away. By using the phrase *we know* Nicodemus is assuming the upper hand on matters of religion. It implies that he (and other members of the Sanhedrin) are the ones who truly know God. *We* are the ones who can make reliable judgments on religious matters, and that extends, in Nicodemus's mind, even to an ability to correctly assess Jesus and his relationship to God. Why else would he claim that he knows that Jesus 'comes from God'?

It needs to be said that some writers, wrongly in my view, have a different take on Nicodemus. They see him as a shy seeker, someone coming to Jesus looking for answers, and under the cover of darkness to hide his embarrassment. They interpret his opening line as setting the scene for a cry for help. However, as we will continue to see, the opening line points in an entirely different direction. Nicodemus arrives expecting to give Jesus some help! We have already been told that Nicodemus was a member of the Sanhedrin and the Pharisees, perhaps the most religiously confident groups in ancient

Judea. It would not be uncommon for one like Nicodemus to address someone like Jesus in the way a seasoned religious teacher would speak to a younger apprentice. *We know* is the phrase that discloses his true outlook. *We know* is what many refer to as the imperial *we*, the academic *we*, the religious *we*. It serves as a gentle reminder that Nicodemus thinks he knows a thing or two about God. What happens next, given that Jesus is only an itinerant preacher, will both surprise and confirm that this was the case.

The first words of Jesus in the conversation are *'Truly, truly, I say to you'*. This phrase is formulaic, and with its double use of *truly*, are not the words of someone trying to help a seeker. Rather, they present a strong challenge to Nicodemus's spiritual confidence. The line is packed with first-century significance. It would be like telling someone: 'Oh really? Well, let me tell you a true thing or two, for it is obvious that you haven't got a clue …'

With it, this much is clear: Jesus takes umbrage at being the object of the Sanhedrin's sage spiritual assessment. In fact, so nonplussed was Jesus that he will go on to repeat this cutting line of challenge twice: 'Truly, truly, I say to you, unless one is born again he cannot see the kingdom of God… Truly, truly, I say to you, unless one is born of water and the Spirit, he cannot enter the kingdom of God.'

Evidently, this start to a conversation with Jesus on religion set off something visceral within him. It opened with a bang! Not only was Jesus offended by the presumption of this religious man, but did you notice the overt warning he levelled against the confidence of people like Nicodemus—the very real danger, in spite of his religious convictions, of falling short of even *seeing* the kingdom of God, let alone *entering* into it. Wow. Jesus has not only questioned Nicodemus's command of religion, but the very relationship with God he thought religion gave him.

OUR OWN RELIGIOUS CONFIDENCE CONSIDERED

We should take a moment at this point in the conversation to reflect on some implications for us. Some important things about religion have already been said. Jesus was convinced that this religious, well-meaning man, was, in no uncertain terms, in danger of missing out on the kingdom of God altogether! Nicodemus's budding confidence, which flowed from his spiritual stature and deeply religious background, was denounced. It was declared to be misplaced. For him, this must have been earth shaking. Even if for us this might be less so. Today, people are generally more flexible in their faith commitments and able to explore other options.

That was not the case for Nicodemus. His beliefs were more fixed. It was haunting to have your belief determined insufficient, and be told that your religion could prohibit you from ever *seeing* the kingdom of God, let alone *entering* it. To think that the one obstacle in coming to a true knowledge of God might very well be your confidence in religion was unimaginable. Your faith entirely misplaced, mistaken, and as a result meaningless and helpless to save.

For those who consider themselves to be religious, by which I mean anyone who thinks of themselves as spiritually inclined and sensitively connected to God, the implication is clear. According to Jesus, your own adherence to religion and spiritual self-perception may not be the most accurate indicator of what constitutes a true relationship with God. It is easy today to count yourself as religious simply because you think about God often. But evidently, this may not be enough. After all, if someone as spiritually sincere as Nicodemus can fall prey to misguided belief, so can we.

Questions now abound. Could it be that many of us need to make the devastating discovery that our embrace of religion might actually be the very thing keeping us from seeing and entering into God's kingdom? Don't years of attending church, studying the Bible or another religious text count for anything? Won't prayer five times a day accrue some benefit? Doesn't cultivating our spiritual side place us in good stead with God? Would Jesus have made the same assessment about us if we had been the one who met him on that day?

Maybe you have one of these questions? Maybe you have *all* of them. But in light of them: What does Jesus want us to know? If we have deluded ourselves, however unintentionally, into thinking that we have God's approval when in fact we don't, where do we go? If not to our religion, how do we find a true connection with God? Nicodemus was about to find out.

RELIGIOUS CONFIDENCE NEEDS SHAKING

It appears that Nicodemus was thrown off balance by Jesus' words. He was confused.

This was probably the first time in decades that his secure sense of being numbered among the faithful had been questioned. As John's narrative resumes, he exposes this disorientation. Nicodemus asks, 'How can a man be born when he is old? Can he enter a second time into his mother's womb and be born? How can these things be?'

This is, admittedly, a tough moment for Nicodemus. No one likes it when their claim to spiritual authenticity is threatened, least of all someone who has followed hard after God (to the best of their abilities) for decades. And yet, with this opening question—'How can a man be born when he is old?'—Nicodemus appears to reveal a state of perplexity. And with his second question, it looks as if he is trying to regain the upper hand, even with a bit of sarcasm thrown in for good measure. 'A second time into his mother's womb, eh?'

Let's pause. This kind of bewilderment, this questioning, as opposed to the practice of declaring, is important. It is humbling. And I have come to think of it as the indispensable in-between place, standing between what was and what may yet be. It is that period of time, or stage in life, that any religious person must come to. It is the kind of place where the ground beneath your belief begins shifting. You feel yourself to be more over water than dry land. No longer assured, and spiritually vulnerable, you find yourself between things. It is this shaking of confidence that Jesus would have Nicodemus embrace. For only then is a person ready to learn. What happens next is remarkable.

HELPFUL WORDS

We have just seen Jesus question Nicodemus's faith more strongly than any of us could have imagined, let alone dared to attempt. But now, with that jarring moment over, and Nicodemus in a curious place, Jesus attempts to steady him toward something better than religion. In addressing the questions Jesus tries to help:

> *'Truly, truly, I say to you, unless one is born of water and the Spirit, he cannot enter the kingdom of God. That which is born of the flesh is flesh, and that which is born of the Spirit is spirit. Do not marvel that I said to you, "You must be born again." The wind blows where it wishes, and you hear its sound, but you do not know where it comes from or where it goes. So it is with everyone who is born of the Spirit.'*

For us, these are strange words to get hold of. We are not at all sure what Jesus is doing with them, or why they come next in the conversation. Yet, perhaps the words Jesus spoke here were chosen because of the common ground they shared with Nicodemus's area of expertise. Remember, this man was a teacher of the Hebrew Bible. He knew God's Word inside and out.

The common ground is revealed by the way that *water, spirit and wind* are used in the context of giving someone a new life with God. Those three words appear together in a book in the Hebrew Bible that Nicodemus would have been very familiar with, even if we aren't. As Nicodemus knew, God promised the prophet Ezekiel that he was in the business of bringing spiritually dead people back to life. In fact, in Ezekiel's most famous of visions (dry bones become living people in Ezekiel chapters 36 and 37), God paints a picture of Israel in the time of the prophet as being religiously dead. They needed to be made alive again, but it would not be by their religion. Rather, it would be by his *Spirit* (or *breath*) which he promises to put within them. Ezekiel said it would be by a cleansing of sin, which he likens to washing them with the *water* of new life. *Water, spirit,* and *wind* (or *breath*, as Ezekiel says).

As a religious teacher, Nicodemus should have known what Jesus was referring to. The clues were all in place. Jesus had put everything out in the open. Nicodemus should have recognized that Jesus wasn't referring to two physical births. Rather, as Ezekiel's vision made clear, the first birth is physical but the second one is spiritual. In essence, Jesus was now alluding, through Ezekiel, to the fact that while we are all born into this world once, if we are to know God for real, it won't come by religion. Instead, it will require being born again by his Spirit.

In speaking to Nicodemus in this way, Jesus has helped us as well. After all, spiritual deadness, as depicted by a field of dry bones, is something we can all envision. It is an apt image, not only for Nicodemus, but for us as well. Ezekiel's vision shows that God must do what our religion cannot. God must wash us. God must breathe new life into us. God must enliven our spirit and replace it with his own.

According to Jesus, religion won't cut it. Good works won't do it. Our moral uprightness has limits. The big takeaway at this point in our conversation with Jesus on religion is this: we all need to be disabused of the belief that we are naturally born into God's family. That we can somehow earn our stay in it, as if a relationship with God comes through heritage or family line, or religious devotion, or the careful cultivation of our spiritual side. No. No matter how sincerely such convictions may be held, Jesus claims that we are born out of sorts with God, and in need of being born again—born again by his Spirit. Our best attempts at living *the moral life* won't be enough to lift us up to God. Like Nicodemus, you and I are in desperate need of something that only comes down from God above.

RELIGIOUS CONFIDENCE NEEDS UNDERSTANDING

Did Nicodemus get all this? Did he connect the dots that Jesus had given him? Would he now ask what must be done to start over again with God? Would he ask how he could receive God's Spirit? Did he understand? It would appear that on this night, he hadn't quite thought his way clear. In ongoing confusion, he simply says to Jesus: 'How can these things be?'

This didn't sit well with Jesus. In a verbal barrage of palpable frustration, Jesus replies: 'Are you the teacher of Israel and yet you do not understand these things?'

In other words: 'I can't help you if you, a teacher of the Bible, don't even know the truths that come from your own religious text.' This was tough love from the young teacher. And it reveals to us that the conversation Nicodemus wanted to have with Jesus on religion wasn't going as planned. If you and I had been there, we would have said that Nicodemus, this well respected, God-fearing, spiritually-minded man, was about to head home that night in a state of complete confusion.

But, Jesus wasn't done. He goes on to castigate Nicodemus, speaking with an imperial *we* of his own. 'I've revealed profound mysteries to you in a way that you should have understood. How could you possibly understand about *being lifted up* and you don't even recognize me as the one who has come down from heaven?'

Nicodemus is completely without confidence or understanding. Uncertain of himself, and of his command of faith—he is at a loss for words. The self-assurance he had in his relationship with God, the careful attention he had given to his behavior, the cultivation of his soul, all these things which had been the hallmarks of his life up to now, have now been disturbed. Like clouds of dust kicked up from the desert floor, Nicodemus has become a man wandering in a spiritual wilderness. Unsettled.

Ironically, and from the perspective of Jesus (given how he is about to conclude the conversation), Nicodemus's state of religious bewilderment was actually preparing him to hear of a better way. And this is not only true for Nicodemus, but for any of us who are unsure where we are heading off to, if not to religion. Take heart! Jesus has one thing more to say. The conversation is not over.

HOPEFUL WORDS

As Nicodemus turned toward the door, now emptied of his confidence in religious status, Jesus said something. He would offer him a line, a word which, in time, had the means of instilling future hope. Pausing, and knowing that he had taken Nicodemus as far as he could on this night, Jesus looked purposefully at him and said:

> '…as Moses lifted up the serpent in the wilderness, so must the Son of Man be lifted up, that whoever believes in him may have eternal life.'

At first glance, these last words by Jesus appear to be a strange conclusion to this conversation on religion. What can they possibly refer to? Why this obscure reference to Moses and the lifting up of a serpent in the wilderness? And what could this visual image have to do with belief and eternal life?

By now it won't surprise you to learn that these hopeful words come from material Nicodemus should have known well. Specifically, they recount another incident in the Bible, but this one occurred during Israel's wandering years in the wilderness after they had escaped from slavery in Egypt. The book of Numbers (chapter 21) records the time when slithering serpents entered the camp as God's instruments of divine wrath for the people's ongoing sin. Many were dying of snake bites. But then, by an act of mercy, God intervened. His righteous act of judgment gave way to an equally powerful act of grace. He told Moses to make a serpent from bronze and to lift it high upon a pole, right in the middle of the camp. And then he told him to instruct those who had been bitten to look at the serpent on the pole. In doing so, they would be healed. No other religious act was needed. Simply by trusting in God's Word, as evidenced by turning toward an object that God raised up, death could be averted. A fresh start in life could be had.

With these hopeful words, coming at the close of his conversation with Nicodemus on religion, Jesus was pointing him to how God saves. The people in the wilderness were not saved by their ongoing adherence to religion. They were not saved by having been born into a religious family. Instead they were rescued (brought into a life-giving relationship with God) by doing what God told them: turning and looking at the *sign* or *symbol* God told Moses to lift up. And as it was for them, so Jesus seems to imply, it can be for Nicodemus, but only in God's good time.

Truth be told though, and from our perspective, it is difficult to see just how this enigmatic moment in Israel's history provides future hope for Nicodemus, let alone for us. Where was he supposed to go from here? What was he to think?

Perhaps it will help to imagine Nicodemus as the door closed behind him that night. Retreating back out into the darkness, his mind would have been racing as he tried to process everything that had been said: 'Well, let me start with what I now know. Jesus ended our conversation by reminding me how one gets a second chance. God's wrath, which was rightly warranted by Israel's sin, must be averted. And any hope of being saved from the deadly bite of the serpents had to come from God alone. Since religion can't do it (after all, everyone dying from a serpent bite was religious!), something else must. A *sign*, or *symbol* of God's grace, had to be given. And when it finally did appear, Israel only needed to take God at his word (that is, to have faith in his promise) by turning toward what he had provided in exchange for sin. When one begins to believe, the effect would be one of being born again, of emerging from the womb a second time, of seeing and entering into the kingdom of God, of possessing all that was needed for eternal life.'

If these were the thoughts that Nicodemus now contemplated, then we are right to ask: What sign can save? And to what, or whom, must we look? If not to religion, then what? What symbol stands in our midst as a tower of hope?

These questions, and more, now belong to us. And yet, on that night, this religious man, who exemplifies so many people today, had no way of knowing just how quickly the sign and symbol that saves us all from sin was about to be given. In this respect, the Gospel of John does not disappoint!

RELIGIOUS CONFIDENCE NEEDS REPLACING

John records that Nicodemus saw Jesus again—many months or even a couple years later. But on that occasion, there would be no opportunity for a conversation. They would not be able to speak with one another, for Jesus had been silenced and crucified on a Roman cross. Whatever help Nicodemus was to receive now would have to come from sight alone. John writes:

> *After these things Joseph of Arimathea, who was a disciple of Jesus, but secretly for fear of the Jews, asked Pilate that he might take away the body of Jesus, and Pilate gave him permission. So he came and took away his body. Nicodemus also, who earlier had come to Jesus by night, came bringing a mixture of myrrh and aloes, about seventy-five pounds in weight. So they took the body of Jesus and bound it in linen cloths with*

*the spices, as is the burial custom of
the Jews.*

This is the scene that concludes what began
as a conversation. Nicodemus, the religious
man who surfaced in the first part of John's
gospel, is still hanging around at the end. He is
mentioned as one of two men who took Jesus
off the cross and buried him in the tomb. It is
not hard for us to imagine Nicodemus now.
Coming up a hill and approaching Jesus on
the cross (not at all like his earlier approach
to the door of an ordinary home), his eyes are
now transfixed on the one who has been *lifted
up*. Blood spilled, body listless, dead. Sign.
Symbol. Twisted on a tree, Jesus, like a serpent
on a pole for all to see.

Ironically, only three days before this terrible
event, Jesus had said: '…when I am lifted
up from the earth, I will draw all people to
myself.' To which John had added, 'He said
this to show by what kind of death he was
going to die.'[3]

Nicodemus is now at last on level ground. He is standing beneath the cross. And we stand there with him. Looking up, he turns his eyes on Jesus, and asks in hushed tones: 'Could it be? What was it that he said to me to me on the night I had my conversation with him? The serpent! Yes, that was it—lifted high upon the pole. God's wrath turned away. Life given. Relationship restored. And now this man, Jesus, lifted up for all to see. And me? Oh my, all my striving to be good; all my devotion to the things of God. I perceive their empty merit. No amount of effort can satisfy for my wayward ways. A substitute is what I need. Jesus. Is atonement now being made for me? Has the certain death of the bite of the serpents now been conquered? And is it dead to me? A perfect sacrifice. God! Send your Spirit down and give me life. Wash me clean. Breathe life into me. For now I see in whom I must believe. Now I enter in.'

His adherence to religion appears to have been replaced by a relationship with Jesus.

AND WHAT ABOUT YOU?

Nicodemus's night-time conversation with Jesus on religion set him off on a time of intense spiritual exploration—one so strong that it held his curiosity to a better end. How did he get there? First, his confidence in religion had been shaken. He was brought to a place where he was without understanding. But then, in further conversation with Jesus he had been helped, and even given words of hope. And in the end, long after the conversation, he was given the opportunity to set his religion aside and embrace a relationship with God by faith. He simply needed to look to Jesus for rescue instead. It would be Jesus' death on the cross that alone overcame his dependence on religious activity.

And what about you?

Are you willing to acknowledge that your own spiritual perception may not be the strongest or most accurate indicator of what constitutes a true relationship with God?

Do you believe that being religious, that is, spiritually open, sensitive, and well meaning, isn't enough to bring you into a relationship with God?

Are you prepared to give yourself to Jesus' understanding of what it takes to know God and living under the rule of his kingdom?

Do you have faith that Jesus' death on the cross was God's final and perfect sacrifice for your sin?

Are you willing to renounce, however noble and religious, your actions and set of beliefs as the things that make for a right relationship with God?

If so, then simply tell God so. And then, set out to find a Bible teaching church that believes these things to help you grow.

JOHN 3:1-15

[1] Now there was a man of the Pharisees named Nicodemus, a ruler of the Jews. [2] This man came to Jesus by night and said to him, 'Rabbi, we know that you are a teacher come from God, for no one can do these signs that you do unless God is with him.' [3] Jesus answered him, 'Truly, truly, I say to you, unless one is born again he cannot see the kingdom of God.' [4] Nicodemus said to him, 'How can a man be born when he is old? Can he enter a second time into his mother's womb and be born?' [5] Jesus answered, 'Truly, truly, I say to you, unless one is born of water and the Spirit, he cannot enter the kingdom of God. [6] That which is born of the flesh is flesh, and that which is born of the Spirit is spirit. [7] Do not marvel that I said to you, "You must be born again." [8] The wind blows where it wishes, and you hear its sound, but you do not know where it comes from or where it goes. So it is with everyone who is born of the

Spirit.' [9] Nicodemus said to him, 'How can these things be?' [10] Jesus answered him, 'Are you the teacher of Israel and yet you do not understand these things? [11] Truly, truly, I say to you, we speak of what we know, and bear witness to what we have seen, but you do not receive our testimony. [12] If I have told you earthly things and you do not believe, how can you believe if I tell you heavenly things? [13] No one has ascended into heaven except he who descended from heaven, the Son of Man. [14] And as Moses lifted up the serpent in the wilderness, so must the Son of Man be lifted up, [15] that whoever believes in him may have eternal life.'

ENDNOTES

1. Jacob Neusner, *A Rabbi Talks with Jesus* (New York: Doubleday, 1993), 53.

2. Nicodemus's encounter with Jesus can be found in full by reading the John 3:1-15. I encourage you to read it. The text can be found on pages 48-49. Unless otherwise marked, all subsequent quotations are from this passage.

3. John 12:32-33.

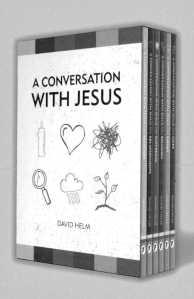

A CONVERSATION
WITH JESUS

DAVID HELM

A CONVERSATION WITH JESUS ON RELIGION
A CONVERSATION WITH JESUS ON SUFFERING
A CONVERSATION WITH JESUS ON DOUBT
A CONVERSATION WITH JESUS ON HOPE

DAVID HELM

A CONVERSATION WITH JESUS
ON RELATIONSHIPS

A CONVERSATION WITH JESUS ON RELATIONSHIPS

She wasn't particularly spiritual. She was looking for something else. A series of failed relationships behind her, she kept hoping for a real connection. Something that would last forever. Something that would satisfy that desire within her.

And then she met Jesus.

Her trip to get water from the well turns into a discussion about living water—and a relationship with the living God. A relationship better than all her previous relationships, that will endure, and give her the satisfaction she has been seeking.

9781527103252

A CONVERSATION WITH JESUS ON SUFFERING

He had been subject to a protracted and excruciating
life of suffering. He was well aware of the unrelenting
persistence of human misery. If anyone had a reason to
feel betrayed by God, this man did.

But then he met Jesus.

At Jesus' command, this man who hasn't walked for 38
years is suddenly on his feet. But this healing brings many
questions. Why this man and not another? Why was he
suffering in the first place? And what would this man do
now he could walk?

9781527103269

A CONVERSATION WITH JESUS ON TRUTH

What is truth? This question, asked by Pilate, a Roman governor in Jerusalem, has echoed down through the centuries and still has ramifications today. His job as representative of Rome and Roman law required that he discover the truth about the charges brought against the prisoner before him.

So he asked Jesus.

The answer Jesus gives and Pilate's reaction are enlightening. The truthfulness of Jesus' words matter. Will you respond in the same way as Pilate?

9781527103276

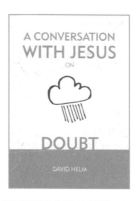

A CONVERSATION WITH JESUS ON DOUBT

Doubt is a virtue—a necessary check on blind certainty. 'Doubting Thomas' is a man who has been known for his doubt throughout history. He was one of Jesus' early followers and he was a man who liked to make up his own mind based on the evidence available to him. When the other disciples told him they'd seen Jesus alive again it sounded outrageous.

But then he saw Jesus.

The evidence of his own eyes, ears, and hands, backed up what his fellow disciples had been saying. But Jesus had a thing or two to say about Thomas' doubt.

9781527103283

A CONVERSATION WITH JESUS ON HOPE

Death is the destroyer of hope. Absence makes itself felt. Plans for the future are demolished. Mary Magdalene knew how this felt. She was devastated. Jesus was dead. His body had disappeared. The hopes that she'd put in him were snuffed out. She stood beside his empty tomb and wept.

But then she met the risen Jesus.

This meeting changes things. If Jesus is alive hope can be reawakened. Death is not victorious. Faith can have meaning. Hope can be yours.

9781527103290

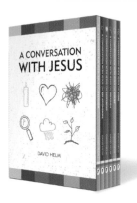

A CONVERSATION WITH JESUS BOXSET

This box contains six short volumes. Six people to meet.
Each appeared on the pages of John's Gospel. Each
met Jesus—the Nazarene, the Christ, the man who
forever changed the world we live in. And each had a
conversation with Jesus about something important to
them. Through these conversations you can meet not only
these six men and women, but the man who changed
everything too.

9781527103238